© ZOE WILSON

RICHARD NELSON
Conversations in Tusculum

Richard Nelson was born in Chicago and attended Hamilton College. He is the recipient of a Tony Award, an Olivier Award for Best Play, two Obie Awards, and a New York Drama Critics' Circle Award, among other honors, as well as a Lila Wallace–Reader's Digest Writing Award and a Guggenheim Fellowship. He is the author of such plays as *Frank's Home, Goodnight Children Everywhere,* and *Some Americans Abroad* and has written or cowritten the book for several musicals, including *Paradise Found, James Joyce's "The Dead,"* and *My Life with Albertine*. In addition, he has translated or adapted classic plays by Chekhov, Strindberg, Pirandello, and Carrière and wrote the screenplay for the film version of Edith Wharton's *Ethan Frome*. He has directed many of his plays on Broadway, off Broadway, in the West End, and in theaters across the country and is at the present time an honorary artistic associate of the Royal Shakespeare Company, which has produced ten of his plays. He lives in upstate New York.

Conversations in Tusculum

CONVERSATIONS IN TUSCULUM

Richard Nelson

FARRAR, STRAUS AND GIROUX

NEW YORK

Farrar, Strauss & Giroux
18 West 18th Street, New York 10011

Printed in the United States of America
First edition, 2008

Library of Congress Cataloging-in-Publication Data
Nelson, Richard, 1950–
    Conversations in Tusculum / Richard Nelson.— 1st ed.
      p.   cm.
    ISBN-13: 978-0-86547-992-0 (pbk. : alk. paper)
    ISBN-10: 0-86547-992-5 (pbk. : alk. paper)
    1. Caesar, Julius—Drama.   2. Rome—History—53–44 B.C.—Drama.   I. Title.

PS3564.E4747C66 2008
812'.54—dc22

                                                              2007051077

Designed by Debbie Glasserman

www.fsgbooks.com

P1

Good men are always happy.

— CICERO

Conversations in Tusculum

PRODUCTION HISTORY

Conversations in Tusculum had its world premiere at the Public Theater (Oskar Eustis, Artistic Director; Mara Manus, Executive Director) in New York City on March 11, 2008. Author/Director: Richard Nelson. Scenic Designer: Tom Lynch. Lighting Designer: Jennifer Tipton. Composer/Sound Designer: John Gromada. Costume Designer: Susan Hilferty. Production Stage Manager: Matthew Silver. Assistant Stage Manager: Jillian Oliver.

BRUTUS	Aidan Quinn
PORCIA	Gloria Reuben
CASSIUS	David Strathairn
SERVILIA	Maria Tucci
CICERO	Brian Dennehy
SYRUS	Joe Grifasi

CHARACTERS

BRUTUS, forties

PORCIA, thirties, his wife and cousin

CASSIUS, forties, his brother-in-law

SERVILIA, late fifties, his mother

CICERO, sixties

SYRUS, forties, an actor

TIME

The play takes place from May 45 B.C. to September
that same year.

SETTING

Tusculum, a small village outside Rome

Tusculum, a town in the Alban Hills, fifteen miles southeast of Rome, is home to many country villas owned by wealthy and politically well-connected Romans.

Scene 1

May. 45 B.C. Brutus's villa in Tusculum. Night. A garden lit by a few oil lamps.

BRUTUS (*forties*) *and* CASSIUS (*forties*) *sit on benches in the garden. They have been drinking and talking for quite some time.*

CASSIUS: I'm not sure what I'd actually expected—

BRUTUS: I'm so pleased we're finally talking about this.

CASSIUS: I'm always thinking about it. Trying to figure it out. What it means. Or meant. What it says about me.

BRUTUS: Me too. So . . .

CASSIUS: So, well, I'd done pretty much everything I could to defeat him and he knew that. But in an odd— He seemed to respect that. Soldier to soldier.

BRUTUS: I know. Does he really mean it?

CASSIUS: Who knows? Then—he pardons me. He asks me for nothing. Treats me like a— One of his own. Does all he can to promote me . . . You lose the feeling that there's ground under your feet, you just . . .

Pause. Off, some dogs bark.

BRUTUS: I've never told this to anyone.

CASSIUS: Neither have—

BRUTUS: What I'm about to say. (*short pause*) After the battle—it was . . . every which way. I—with a few men— we waded into a swamp. And through the whole night we sort of walked? Pushed our way? Swam? Toward Caesar. To surrender? I don't know what I could have been expecting. (*short pause*) At his camp—they don't kill me right away. I assume they'll want—to show me off. They throw me into a small room. No light. I'm there for—I don't know: half a day? Then—he walks in. Breastplate polished, helmet in his hands. No one with him. He closes the door. There's hardly any light at all—except through the cracks in the wall of that hut, and the door. He says, "I understand you asked to clean yourself, Brutus—for me. Before meeting me. But I want to see you like this. Covered in mud and filth." (*short pause*) I tried to stand. "Stay there. On the ground. Your mother," he says. "I've written her. To tell her you're alive. She's asked about a hundred times. Servilia is a good woman—we're both lucky men . . ." Then he's behind me and he sort of knees me in the head. "Why?" he shouts at me. "Why did you do this, Brutus? Since when did you want to become a soldier? What happened to your books? To say nothing—of your investments."

Pause. BRUTUS *looks at* CASSIUS.

I'm not a greedy man.

CASSIUS: Of course not. He knows—

BRUTUS: I'm an honest man!

CASSIUS: He knows how to make us feel small. Feel like nothing.

BRUTUS: Then I think he kicked me in the side of the face, and I'm lying down. "For god's sake—Pompey killed your own father! Why side with such a man? With him over me?! I have been kind."

Short pause.

CASSIUS: Did you try to answer him?

BRUTUS *nods.*

BRUTUS: "I thought it was the right thing to do—for my country," I said. "Which is greater than any one of us. Where no man—is master." No one answers him back now.

CASSIUS: No.

BRUTUS: So he looks at me, and then: "So I should just pardon you? That's why you waded all night through a swamp? Someone so close, so close to me—someone who has—betrayed me?" (*pause*) "That was a question," he says. "What happens to me," I say, "I leave to Caesar."

(*short pause*) "I should slit your throat, then. Or perhaps," he continued, "as you are now such a man of principle— whatever that means—I could just leave a sword behind." I nodded and held out my hand for the sword.

CASSIUS: You did?

BRUTUS: At least I did that. "No," he says. "No, I will keep you alive—not because of your mother and the love and respect I have for her. Alive. And—promote you." Just like with you.

Pause.

CASSIUS: It's good to know I'm not alone.

BRUTUS: Then to seal the deal, to put me permanently in his—debt? His purse? To own me like a slave.

CASSIUS: We are all now Caesar's slaves.

BRUTUS: He tells me, "Pompey, I've learned, is on his way to Egypt. I shall chase him there and spread the word—that it was you who told me this, who'd betrayed him."

CASSIUS: You didn't?

BRUTUS: No.

CASSIUS: Everyone thinks you—

BRUTUS: I know. I know. "And," he says, "outside this hut are five hundred prisoners, good men, some who fought with you, Brutus. Some who waded through that swamp last night with you. Excellent men. Worth their weight in gold. I want one out of every ten killed. As a lesson. Sever the heads, cut off the hands. Not necessarily in that order. Marcus Brutus, my dear friend, my new ally—I want you to choose who lives and who dies. Here's the list. Make your mark." And he lets the paper float to the floor. I watch it. It seems to take forever. I hear footsteps and the door close behind him. A captain was there a second later—requesting my orders. (*short pause*) I tried to find some criteria to— Age? Number of children? I tried a lottery. The more I worked at this, the more I just smelled the rotting stench of Caesar on me. I don't sleep much anymore.

CASSIUS: But then again, we are alive. Pompey would never have been so generous to—

BRUTUS: If "generous" is the word. Perhaps the word is "cruel." I don't know. I don't know. (*pause*) It must be the country air.

CASSIUS: What must?

BRUTUS: Would we ever have spoken like this in Rome? No one's listening here. No one passing by. Here in Tusculum things seem clearer. Or maybe it's just the relief of talking about it.

CASSIUS: (*looking around*) It is nice. You can forget that all this is here—waiting . . .

BRUTUS: I don't think I ever want to go back to Rome.

CASSIUS: Maybe I'll stay longer.

BRUTUS: Do. Send for your son. Do some fishing. Teach him something. Remind yourself—that you're living.

Pause. Dogs bark again.

CASSIUS: I should go; it's very late. If I'm going to get any sleep tonight—

BRUTUS: It's too late, stay here—

CASSIUS: I have my dogs. It's a short walk over the hill.

BRUTUS: I'll get someone to—

CASSIUS: I'm fine. Please. The walk will maybe sober me.

BRUTUS: Is that what we are—drunk?

CASSIUS: I'm sorry to have missed Cicero. Something must have come up along the way.

Dogs louder. PORCIA (*thirties*) *enters.*

PORCIA: He's just arrived.

BRUTUS: Now? At this hour? He shouldn't have been on the road now.

PORCIA: He's here.

CASSIUS: (*at the same time*) It's late for me. I'll come back in the morning—

BRUTUS: Stay and—

PORCIA: He knew we were expecting him.

CASSIUS: (*to* BRUTUS) No, no. I can see this evening's just getting started again. I couldn't— I must get to bed. I'll be back. Good night. Good night.

He starts to hurry off, stops.

And thank you—for urging me to come out here. To the countryside. You are right, I think it does help us see things—clearer.

He hurries off.

PORCIA: (*as* BRUTUS *starts to stand*) No need to rush. Cicero's talking with Syrus, who heard the dogs. And catching up on all the Roman gossip.

BRUTUS *stands.*

Will he be safe getting home?

BRUTUS: He has his dogs. And how is Cicero? How does he seem?

PORCIA: (*stating the obvious*) Like a man who's lost his only daughter.

They go, as dogs bark off.

Scene 2

That same night. A room in BRUTUS*'s villa.* SYRUS (*forties*), *a houseguest and actor, and* CICERO (*sixties*), *who has just arrived, enter talking.*

SYRUS: So he's offered five hundred thousand.

CICERO: Amazing.

SYRUS: To take the stage *himself.*

CICERO: I understand.

SYRUS: To *speak*—in public, what he's written.

CICERO: As a citizen of Rome he can't—

SYRUS: Of course. Caesar knows this. Liberius will lose his citizenship. Social standing. But—five hundred thousand. *And* the risk of turning down Caesar.

CICERO: Which is a real risk.

SYRUS: Caesar knows how to make a deal.

CICERO: Yes. Yes, he does. He knows how to do that. I've known that for a long time.

SYRUS: So Liberius picks a role for himself—the slave.

CICERO: (*smiling*) Good for him. We are all now Caesar's—

SYRUS: Yes. That's becoming a cliché now.

CICERO: Is it? I've been away too long.

SYRUS: When he makes his "entrance"—and we see, by his mask, what he's chosen to play . . . It was like a riot. Cheers. Shouting.

CICERO: And Caesar?

SYRUS: He smiled. He accepted the "joke." Or the . . . (*shrugs*) Liberius was shaking in his boots, his voice cracking. You could hear your own breathing when he as the slave started to speak: "Oh Citizen, you too have lost your liberty."

CICERO: Huh. Good. When was this?

SYRUS: Just before Caesar left for Spain.

CICERO: I hadn't heard any of this. Keep going.

SYRUS: And we all look at Caesar. I look at Liberius, who's sweating buckets now. His eyes—focused right on Caesar, as if to say: you humiliate me, this is what you get back. A great, great moment for us actors. (*short pause*) Of course Caesar doesn't give him the prize.

CICERO: No.

SYRUS: But he pays him. And *then* in front of everyone—he says to Liberius that he can have his position back. Like that—he's a citizen again.

CICERO: You can't just— Caesar can't—

SYRUS: He can. He did. The final humiliation—he gives and he takes.

CICERO: Does he? Liberius must have—

SYRUS: He accepted. (*shrugs*) But then he went abroad. Right away. He's staying away from Rome.

CICERO: Wise.

SYRUS: Even with Caesar in Spain—

CICERO: Wise.

SYRUS: Not a good time—to be an actor.

CICERO: Which explains, Syrus, why you're—

SYRUS: I'm a houseguest. The perennial houseguest. You don't happen to have room in *your* house? (*laughs*)

CICERO: I haven't been there yet, but—

SYRUS: I wasn't really asking. I'm here today. Next week? Next month—Cassius has been kind enough . . .

Short pause. CICERO *has been lost in thought, then he hears what* SYRUS *has just said.*

CICERO: He's in Tusculum as well? Cassius? He rarely comes here. He hates the country.

BRUTUS *enters.*

BRUTUS: Cicero! How well you look!

CICERO: Brutus.

They hug.

You lie. Thank you for lying.

BRUTUS: You looked—rested. That's what I meant. You received my letters?

CICERO: I am sorry I didn't write back—

BRUTUS: (*over this*) I didn't expect— (*looks at him*) It was a great loss. She was a beautiful woman, your daughter.

CICERO: She was. And the baby died too. They wrote me this.

BRUTUS: We know.

They don't know what to say. Short pause.

SYRUS: I should leave you two friends alone—

BOTH: No, no—

CICERO: Please.

BRUTUS: (*to say something*) We thought you'd be earlier.

CICERO: I'm sorry— The roads were— Where is everyone going?

BRUTUS: (*over this*) You shouldn't travel the roads at night.

CICERO: What's going to happen to me?

BRUTUS: My wife said she thought you were soldiers. When she heard you arrive.

CICERO: Why would soldiers—?

BRUTUS: (*shrugs*) It's the middle of the night? That's when soldiers come? (*after a moment*) She worries too much.

CICERO: Congratulations on your marriage. (*to* SYRUS) That— I heard about.

BRUTUS: What can we get you?

CICERO: Nothing. There's nothing I want anymore.

CICERO *is distracted.* BRUTUS *turns to* SYRUS.

BRUTUS: You were catching him up on the gossip?

SYRUS: About Liberius—

BRUTUS: That's old—

SYRUS: He hadn't heard.

CICERO: (*interrupting*) Cassius is here? He never leaves Rome.

BRUTUS: He just left. He came tonight. To see you.

CICERO: Why did he—leave?

BRUTUS: He's coming back in the morning.

CICERO: (*not listening, mostly to himself*) I suppose his wife made him come. (*to* BRUTUS) You two grew up here—

BRUTUS: My sister's in Spain.

CICERO *is confused.* BRUTUS *looks to* SYRUS, *then to* CICERO.

You don't know?

CICERO: What?

BRUTUS: In Spain—with Caesar. My mother "organized" it. He'd especially asked for her. And she went.

CICERO: Cassius let his wife do this?

BRUTUS: Cassius didn't know what to do. Junia decided for both of them. It was safest, she felt, for her to go. They have a son.

CICERO: I know. I know. So . . . I'm trying to understand all this. So . . . Cassius was here.

BRUTUS: And coming back. Tomorrow. I suggested he bring the son from Rome. And do things. I can't imagine what it's like in Rome for Cassius right now. Maybe I should let you go to bed—

Tries to take CICERO *by the elbow.* CICERO *shakes his head.*

(*to say something*) Syrus has been staying—

SYRUS: I told him.

BRUTUS: Very useful to have an actor in the house.

CICERO: (*a serious question*) Why?

BRUTUS: Good company. Always has something to say. Don't you? Don't you?

SYRUS: (*getting the hint, to* CICERO) How was the—trip? Took—a long time?

BRUTUS *just looks at* SYRUS. CICERO *is still lost in his own thoughts.*

(*another try*) How's your young wife? I'll bet she's missed you.

CICERO: I'm trying to get rid of her. Of that mistake. She's in my villa now, I understand. Tomorrow morning I'll need someone to get her out. I don't want to see her. I don't want to be reminded of my mistakes. Do you think your wife, Brutus, could do that?

BRUTUS: I'll ask.

CICERO: She could talk to her. Move her along.

BRUTUS: I'm sure she will.

CICERO: It'll be hard enough just walking in there.

For the first time in the scene, he sits. Pause.

I don't sleep anymore.

BRUTUS: Who does? Porcia never sleeps.

CICERO: Then you'll keep me company?

BRUTUS: Of course. (*He sits.*)

CICERO: Syrus, maybe you're tired—

SYRUS: No, no. (*He sits.*)

CICERO: I wept for days. I didn't even dare think of return-ing—to here. She died here. It was like, Brutus, a wall col-lapsing, or levee, and then the flood. I surprised myself at the depth and extent of my pain. Of course I knew I loved my daughter—so very much. I knew the joy I took in her company. More than with anyone. But grief, even in this dimension, it passes, doesn't it? Time covers it up. And we get better. (*short pause*) This I know. But let me tell you— I suddenly realized, having the daughter taken away— (*looks to them*) That this world. Our country. One could ignore things, accept them—because we were looking ahead for our children. To make it all better for them. Let's live through this. Let's survive that. For our children. It's how I'd come to explain things to myself. But my child is dead. And what I am left with is what we have—not what we hope to become. The death of our children—it asks us the question: not what will we be, this country, but rather only what have we become? So I wept. For the first few months for my daughter, then maybe for me. Then for our nation, this Republic, and I haven't been able to stop. And I knew staying away wasn't going to help. *This* wasn't going to heal.

BRUTUS: You have your son.

CICERO: A crass, stupid young man who adores Caesar. I had to bribe him to keep him from running off to Spain. (*pause*) I'm alone. And the world we have—is all I'll ever know. (*short pause*) He wrote me a nice letter. Caesar. About my daughter. He wrote from Spain. He found the time. I was impressed.

BRUTUS: It's all gone well there for him.

CICERO: It has.

BRUTUS: Well, and he'd lost a daughter himself so—

CICERO: I suppose. (*short pause*) But I have to say—I was suspicious. Whatever he does now, I'm suspicious. I figure there's always another reason. He's always after something, to do something, prove—humiliate? I imagined while down south having a conversation with him. Just us. Like we used to. A little gossip. Talk. Discussion. Even argument. I tried to hear his voice. But I can't remember it now. All I kept thinking is: Cicero, watch what you say. Careful.

BRUTUS: His Egyptian whore's still in Rome.

CICERO: I've heard this.

BRUTUS: With his bastard. "Caesarion." She has a sense of humor.

CICERO: She does that. (*smiles*) A wicked one.

BRUTUS: When he comes back—there's talk it'll be proposed that he become Dictator for Life.

CICERO: I've heard even worse. Moving the capital to Alexandria. Anything—to keep us all in our place. And have a little sport with us. Of us. I've been writing. Down south. Nothing else to do.

BRUTUS: That's good news.

CICERO: I paid for a copy (*nods to* BRUTUS) for you. It's with my things.

BRUTUS: I shall look forward to it.

CICERO: *Self-Consolation.* The title. I wrote it to feel better.

BRUTUS: I write for the same reason. Some days I think it's all we can do, all that's left to us—write. And write. And write. As long as we don't show it to anyone. Or just to friends.

PORCIA *has entered and stands at a distance, unseen by the others.*

SYRUS: I performed something Brutus wrote tonight at dinner.

PORCIA: He wrote it for his friend.

They turn and see her.

CICERO: (*surprised*) Brutus has written a play?

BRUTUS: A few speeches—

CICERO: (*continuing*) A playwright like Caesar!

SYRUS: I hear he's stopped.

CICERO: Has he.

BRUTUS: It was meant to be for you—tonight. Your return. In your honor. Cassius was here, we were waiting, we did it anyway, for him.

PORCIA: Syrus could give it to him.

BRUTUS: It's too late.

CICERO: (*over this*) I don't sleep.

PORCIA: Let him hear it.

CICERO: (*to* BRUTUS) And it's about—?

PORCIA: My father.

CICERO: Cato.

PORCIA: His death. (*to* SYRUS) I'll get you your mask. (*She hurries off.*)

CICERO: (*to* BRUTUS) I thought you disagreed with suicide. Against your beliefs.

BRUTUS: In most cases, I do.

CICERO: But Cato's?

BRUTUS: I don't know. Most days now—I wish I'd done the same.

CICERO: There's still time.

BRUTUS: I don't know. Isn't it too late?

PORCIA *enters with* SYRUS's *mask, gives it to him. He puts it on.*

(*to* CICERO) You're sure you want to—

CICERO: Yes.

BRUTUS: You've been traveling—

CICERO: Please!

PORCIA *stands at a distance and watches.*

BRUTUS: (*giving the background*) Cato in Utica, he—

CICERO: I know what happened.

BRUTUS: As Caesar advances against him . . .

SYRUS *stands in the middle of the room.*

He's alone in his room.

SYRUS: (*in mask*)
"Do you think to keep a man of my age alive
by force, and to sit here and silently watch me?
Or do you bring some reasons to prove,
that it will not be base and unworthy of Cato,
when he can find his safety, no other way,
to seek it from—his enemy? If so,
let them advance their arguments now,
show cause why I should now unlearn what
I formerly was taught, in order that rejecting
all convictions, I may now by Caesar's help and grace
grow wiser, and be yet more obliged to him for life.

"Listen, to dispatch myself I need no sword,
I need but hold my breath
or strike my head against that wall. My sword!"

BRUTUS: A slave boy brings him his sword.

BRUTUS *hands* SYRUS *a pretend sword.*

And then leaves him.

Pause.

SYRUS: "Now—I am master of myself.
For those who conquered, entreat, and those
who have done wrong, beg pardon.
For myself, I do not confess to any defeat
in all my life, but rather so far as I have

thought fit I have got the victory and have
conquered Caesar in all points of justice and honesty!
It is Caesar that ought to be looked upon
as one surprised and vanquished,
for he is now convicted and found guilty
of those designs against my country.

"Hence, here is my answer, my life.
For to be preserved by Caesar's favor,
I should myself go to him,
and I would be beholden not just to the tyrant
but to his acts of tyranny.

"Once great Rome, a beacon in the sky;
without freedom, let me die.
Knowing the good man only is free,
and all wicked men are slaves."

He stabs himself with the pretend sword and dies.

Silence. No one has anything to say. SYRUS *slowly stands up, brushing off his clothes.* PORCIA *suddenly hurries from the room, upset.*

BRUTUS: (*explaining*) He was her father.

CICERO: And your uncle. (*pause*) And Cato's villa here in Tusculum? What has happened to that? Confiscated, I assume.

BRUTUS *shrugs.*

You have Cato speak like he's addressing the Republic of Plato. When in fact, Brutus, he needs to be speaking to us—the scum of Rome.

BRUTUS: I will go and get us some wine. If we're staying up all night, I need to keep drinking.

CICERO: I haven't started.

BRUTUS: Then you'll have to catch up.

BRUTUS *goes. Short pause.*

CICERO *reaches over to* SYRUS *and takes his mask.*

CICERO: (*to* SYRUS, *as he looks at the mask*) What else has changed since I've been gone? How lost have we become?

Scene 3

The next day, late morning. Hillside, overlooking CICERO*'s villa* (*unseen*), *Tusculum.*

Three camp stools. CICERO, BRUTUS, *and* CASSIUS *sit or stand. They have been waiting and are in the middle of a conversation.* CASSIUS *holds a book.*

BRUTUS: (*turning pages in the book in* CASSIUS*'s hand*) Now read—(*finds the place*) that part.

CASSIUS: (*reads*) "Grief is not a condition of the senses, but of the soul. And the physician need put away his tools before administering to such a patient. Who cries and laments from a source like that of a place far away, unexplored. It cries like beasts in a song never heard. For days I wept at the loss of my daughter—"

CASSIUS *looks to* CICERO, *who is staring off across the country-side.*

(*continues after a look to* BRUTUS) "—For days I wrote these words through wet eyes. I looked for comfort in old books and in nature. I learned this: grief is not a passion that can be comforted. We must express it in all its force, in all we have lost . . ." (*He closes the book. Then, to* BRUTUS) Was there another—?

BRUTUS: No, that was the last one. Though I'm sure there are many more.

CASSIUS *tries to hand the book to* BRUTUS.

I think that's yours.

CICERO *nods.*

He gave me my copy last night. I've only started reading it, but I thought those passages—

CASSIUS: Yes. Thank you. (*looks the book over*) *Self-Consolation* . . . ?

Smiles to himself, then to CICERO.

Thank you.

CICERO *looks at him and shrugs, as if to say, it is nothing.*

Then (*half to himself, as he pats the book*) I shall read it all with great interest. (*to* CICERO) My wife's in Spain. Did you know?

No response.

CICERO: (*to* BRUTUS) Your wife's taking a long time. What's Porcia doing?

BRUTUS: The girl I'm sure thinks it's her house. She thinks you're her husband. It takes time to explain things.

Short pause.

CASSIUS: (*to* CICERO) I have friends who say that his (*nods toward* BRUTUS) marriage was the most courageous thing they'd seen in a long time. That it'd given them some hope. That we could still fight back—

BRUTUS: I married a wife. Nothing more—

CASSIUS: He thinks he owns us then—

BRUTUS: Cassius—

CASSIUS: I wonder what Caesar thought. I would have liked to have seen his face when he heard. He must have believed he'd had you completely under his control, in his debt, but you found a way—

BRUTUS: I wasn't looking for a way—

CASSIUS: (*to* CICERO) Look at him. He can't keep a straight face!

BRUTUS: (*smiling*) I only got married.

CASSIUS: (*to* CICERO) To Cato's daughter! That went through town like an explosion. Caesar couldn't help but see that as a slap in the face. He did something.

BRUTUS: (*over the end of this, to* CICERO) What did I do?!! What did I do?!! What can we do?!

CASSIUS: (*shouting at the same time, to* CICERO) He did something!!! He did something!!!

Short pause.

(*to* BRUTUS) I'm trying to praise you.

BRUTUS: I don't deserve praise. (*to* CICERO) My wife and I are enjoying ourselves here. I'm thinking we could live full-time in the country.

CASSIUS: I didn't know that. Why would you do that?

BRUTUS: I just told you, we—just like it here.

CASSIUS: Are you scared to live in—

BRUTUS: No! I'm not scared!

Pause.

CICERO: My daughter knew it was a mistake. My marriage to this girl. I should have listened. But she came with money. A lot of it. I needed money. Now I don't care about that.

CASSIUS: How old is she again—twelve? (*smiles at* BRUTUS)

CICERO: Seventeen. When I divorced her, my wife was like an animal. She went for my throat.

BRUTUS: You were marrying a child.

CICERO: An old man's infatuation, she said. She ran around to all my friends: the old ass is marrying a girl. Did she—? (*looks at* CASSIUS *and* BRUTUS)

CASSIUS *and* BRUTUS *both nod.*

You know what I said? I said, "Well, she'll be a woman by tomorrow!" (*laughs*)

The others don't laugh.

Pause.

She'd been my ward. Came to me when she was thirteen. One day there's this young woman. Whatever I said, whatever came out of my mouth—she found thrilling. After my wife—well, you understand. I was susceptible. Tullia kept saying: she's too young, Father. She needs to "ripen." What makes us think—us men think—that that is a process we help with—can expedite? She laughed at everything. (*pause*) When Tullia died—she . . . I suppose, to be fair, if you've had no life, you can't really understand or feel tragedy. If you haven't had something—that is then taken away—you can't feel the depth of loss. A child's tears—it's why they can sometimes make one smile. But an old man's tears—those tears are never humorous. (*short pause*) She felt nothing I felt. She understood nothing. It even crossed my mind that she was somehow relieved that my daughter would no longer be a— What? An obstacle? Competitor? I don't know. What do girls think? I looked at her—literally the day my daughter died—I looked and saw a young woman whom I despised. Can there be anything worse in the world than to be saddled with someone who has not even the capacity, let alone the will, to understand you? (*short pause*)

I hope she's packing her things . . . (*He stands and looks off.*) She'll want her dowry back.

Turns and looks at BRUTUS.

BRUTUS: She will.

CICERO: I'll have to mortgage something. Or sell it off. (*pause*) What is taking so long? I want to go home. (*looks off*) Antony's been attacking me. He's been the worst.

BRUTUS: I heard. You can't—

CICERO: Agrees with Tullia's mother. I'm supposed to be a pervert. Who likes little girls. For god sake, she's a woman! And this from a drunkard like— Who's billeting with a harem of actresses. Has he no shame?

BRUTUS: The war in Spain has gone well for "us." "Them." They have no one else to fight. "We've" won. And so without a war, perhaps Caesar will—

CICERO: He won't.

BRUTUS: No.

CASSIUS: You've heard about the statue?

BRUTUS: Cassius—

CICERO: (*at the same time*) What??

CASSIUS: He should know what it's like now. What we've become. Caesar's put up a statue—of Cleopatra. Next to Venus. He's made her a goddess.

CICERO: (*incredulous*) No.

CASSIUS: And if she's a goddess—what does that make Caesar? At least in his mind.

BRUTUS: (*looking off*) Here comes Porcia.

CICERO: (*trying to see*) Is she alone? I can't talk to that girl.

BRUTUS: She's alone.

They are standing. CASSIUS *picks up the book.*

CASSIUS: I look forward to reading this—

CICERO: (*what has been on his mind*) Listen to me, both of you. (*He looks off.*) Before she gets here. This girl—my "wife"— she is probably going to say that we never . . . And the truth is—we didn't. I didn't. I couldn't. The two times I tried—it did not happen. She can make me into a laughingstock.

PORTIA *enters.*

PORCIA: She's agreed.

CICERO: Thank you. Thank all of you.

PORCIA: There. Look. (*She points off.*) That's her and her people. I made sure she left. I waited until she was out. She wants her dowry back. I told her fine.

CICERO: I'll find the money.

CASSIUS: What about her virginity? She can't get that back, can she? (*He looks to* CICERO *and laughs, nods.*)

PORCIA: (*hesitates, then*) No, I guess not. And she certainly didn't say anything about that.

CICERO: Good.

PORCIA: I suppose she knows better—but she certainly is young. (*to* CICERO) What could you have been thinking?

CICERO: I don't know. I don't know. So— (*He gets up.*) I can go home now.

PORCIA: She broke some things.

CICERO: My art?

PORCIA: Be prepared.

CASSIUS: I'll go with you.

CASSIUS *and* CICERO *start to go.*

CICERO: (*to* CASSIUS) My home is full of ghosts.

CASSIUS: Here, hold my arm.

CICERO: (*as he takes* CASSIUS*'s arm, and as they go*) Tullia died there. And the baby. I sat outside and heard my daughter's screams. I sat here . . .

They are gone. PORCIA *sighs and sits, exhausted.* BRUTUS *looks off.*

PORCIA: God, where do these little girls come from? Who think they're women? When I was her age, I knew nothing about negotiations. I accepted what was proposed. It was up to my family.

BRUTUS: What did she want?

PORCIA: She threatened—she says they never slept toge- ther. Successfully. (*She looks to* BRUTUS.) Is that what he says?

No response.

She said—she'd make him out to be the biggest fool. That's where she began. I said, if you can't excite an old man who probably hasn't slept with a woman in years— what does that say about you, my dear? So it quickly just became about money. Prestige, which is money. Prop- erty—also just money. Money, that's all that matters to anyone anymore. "How much can I get?" So we came up with a number. He'll have to come up with it to keep her off his back. (*sighs*) Did I do all right?

He nods.

Thank you. I feel like I need to wash. I don't understand why he couldn't just have done that himself.

BRUTUS: (*looking off*) Because—he's a coward? (*he turns to her; what's been on his mind*) I must go back to Rome to- morrow. I'll stay no longer than I have to. Then—I'm thinking I'd like to stay here for the whole summer. Not go anywhere.

PORCIA: Stay here??

BRUTUS: Syrus went out early to fish. I like to fish. What do you think we should do? (*no response*) I'm asking what you think. (*pause*) You always look scared. What are you so frightened of? (*short pause*) Cicero talked for hours last night about your father. Said Cato was the only man he'd ever known who was greater than his reputation. He says—you look like him, Porcia. When your father was young. Cicero says he looks at you and he sees . . . So— another reminder that we aren't the man your father was. As if we needed another reminder. (*He stands to go.*)

PORCIA: I think you look scared too.

Short pause.

BRUTUS: I didn't sleep at all last night.

PORCIA: You were up all night talking.

BRUTUS: Yes. (*He starts to go.*)

PORCIA: That is something we do very well, isn't it?

BRUTUS: What?

PORCIA: Talk.

He goes, she follows.

Scene 4

Hillside on CICERO's *property, Tusculum. His villa [unseen] in the distance. Afternoon, summer, birds. Two months have passed; July.*

CICERO *sits.* SERVILIA (*late fifties*), BRUTUS's *mother, has just arrived from Rome.*

CICERO: It's been a while.

SERVILIA: It has. You're looking well.

CICERO: Lie better. Still, each day it gets a little—duller.

SERVILIA: I'm sorry—

CICERO: Don't. Condolences—I have had enough to last a lifetime. Even your "friend" Caesar wrote. Very nice of him.

SERVILIA: He'd also lost a daughter.

CICERO: Oh. Then that's why. He "understands." (*pause*) They're fishing. (*He gestures off.*)

SERVILIA: That's all I hear my son does now.

CICERO: (*over this*) Go and . . .

She doesn't move.

Does your son know you were coming?

She shakes her head, then looks around and off.

SERVILIA: I spent my childhood here. In these hills. I learned to sew here. Shear sheep. Ride a donkey. I could stay here forever.

(*She hands* CICERO *a letter.*)

CICERO: What's this?

SERVILIA: From my son. It arrived this week.

He reads the letter. A flock of birds flies by.

How beautiful it is here. (*indicating the letter*) I thought he was here—relaxing. It's that new wife of his. That (*gestures toward the letter*) is her influence. How she thinks.

He finishes and tries to hand the letter to her. She won't take it.

CICERO: Burn it. Forget about it.

SERVILIA: My excuse for coming is that I'm to sell my brother's villa.

CICERO: (*nods, then*) And what would your brother, Cato, have thought about that, I wonder.

SERVILIA: He'd have thought—get a good price. (*She smiles.*) I will sit down. (*She sits.*) He's safe down there?

CICERO: He's with Cassius and Cassius's son. And your new daughter-in-law. (*He smiles.*)

SERVILIA: "The family." (*short pause*) My brother and I—when he wasn't in school, which was where he was most of the time—we'd play together here. And when Brutus was a boy, I brought him here as often as I could. Get him out of Rome. Rome's not fit for a child.

CICERO: No.

SERVILIA: Nor for anyone with any innocence left.

Short pause.

CICERO: (*pointedly*) Is your daughter back from Spain?

She doesn't respond.

SERVILIA: Why don't you buy the villa? I hear you're looking for a place for your daughter's shrine.

CICERO: With what? Look at me. And that little girl I married wants all of her dowry back—

SERVILIA: (*pointedly*) From what I hear, you can't blame her for—

CICERO: (*interrupting*) How much are you looking for? For Cato's villa?

She shrugs.

Let me help set a price. After all, it'll affect what mine's worth as well.

SERVILIA: (*interested*) You're thinking of selling?

CICERO: No. No. I couldn't. How could I? My daughter died here. Such a sunny day. But the sun doesn't seem to matter anymore. (*then about the letter he is still holding*) What's strange about his letter—your son and I have had endless talks. He's always taken the side that killing yourself wasn't a course. Your brother's suicide as well. We've sat out here and argued— He still believes—

SERVILIA: What? What does he believe?

CICERO: I'm not sure. But he thought Cato was wrong. He should have *fought* and died. Surrounded? Then face Caesar. Make Caesar the one who . . . The blood on his hands. But don't end your own life. I disagreed. It was a healthy argument. I've held a knife to my throat at least five times these past few months. Everything that was, I see is now gone. He's heard me . . . And now I fear I've convinced Brutus— When it's been his arguments that have saved me. (*short pause*) There are moments, Servilia, when one's own death—given all that one witnesses now in the world—one's own demise seems to be the happiest route. To somewhere. I understand this. I'm saddened by this (*indicating the letter*). I won't burn it.

SERVILIA: Talk to him, Cicero. That's why I'm here. He needs to listen to someone besides that wife.

CICERO *folds the letter and puts it away.*

CICERO: Suicide—it has its good points. (*smiles*) I know—
sometimes you feel like just breathing the air makes you
guilty, culpable—a part of—all this, which we once loved,
this country that—we had so much pride in.

SERVILIA: There's exile.

CICERO: There is. Actually, Brutus must be thinking of this as
well. This morning he told me he'd heard from his friend
Marcellius—who's in exile in Mitylene. He says he's per-
fectly happy there. Doesn't miss Rome. He fishes too. Has
horses. Grapes. Wheat. I know I'd rather die first. To be
cut off from what you are. To surrender. Even in death
Cato fights for our souls—we could be like him.

Beat.

If I were like him. Which I'm not. (*short pause*) We are
slaves now—to your lover.

SERVILIA: He's not my lover anymore.

CICERO: No. He's your old lover, who asked you to give him
your daughter—my good friend Cassius's wife—and you
did. Now, there is something to kill yourself over.

She looks at him and stands.

SERVILIA: You don't understand.

CICERO: Oh, I understand. We all in our own way find our
ways to keep going. Cassius fishes with his son. And thinks
about nothing. (*short pause*) I've found my own way.

He leans down and pulls a book from a bag.

Here. I've just finished writing this. My third book in two
months. I just write. This one—appropriately—is about
the glories of study. Of losing oneself in one's mind. Sitting alone—far from the flying spears, bloodied limbs—
and the politics. This gets me through or onto the next
day. My words. My poetry. My thoughts. I live in a mind
far, far richer than anything I see. Where people are more
honest with themselves, where our leaders are not crazed,
crude destroyers of talk, and thought and speech. I've
lived a life in Rome. Now I live here. And work here. And
listen to the insects and the summer breezes and the rain.
(*short pause*) I'm giving Brutus a copy. (*shrugs*) If I could
sit out here and find a way to close a door and keep all
that other out—I would. The world looks so much better
in here (*points to his head; then short pause*) Well, I'm surprised Caesar even allows you to sell your brother's villa.
He could have just leveled it.

SERVILIA: Yes.

CICERO: Cato was his enemy.

SERVILIA: Yes.

CICERO: He could have had it taken down stone by stone. To
make his point. He loves surprising us. (*short pause*) I
knew your brother when we were boys.

SERVILIA: I know. I remember.

CICERO: And you. The skinny little sister. (*smiles*) Cato'd invite me out here. I didn't have a villa then—I got this with my wife's money. I didn't have much, not like . . . (*gestures toward her*) I was in awe of him, of your family. Your history, all you'd done. It's the reason I bought land here, in Tusculum, I suppose—to be close . . . That was such a long time ago. (*He closes his eyes.*)

PORCIA *enters and stops.* ·

PORCIA: (*on seeing* SERVILIA) When did you arrive? We weren't expecting—

CICERO: She just got here.

PORCIA: I was just— They're fishing. There's not much to watch.

SERVILIA: I wouldn't think so.

PORCIA: I was going home. But I should tell my husband that his mother's here.

She hurries off.

SERVILIA: (*calling*) Don't bother him if he's— (*to* CICERO) She's gone.

CICERO: His new wife. (*He smiles at* SERVILIA.)

SERVILIA: That was a mistake. Why didn't he ask me first? Like Brutus taking his fist and shoving it into Caesar's face.

CICERO: Perhaps—that was the point.

SERVILIA: Then it was a stupid point to make. And she's a very stupid woman.

CICERO: She's well-read. She's read me.

SERVILIA: We're talking different things.

CICERO: (*looking off*) They're all coming now.

SERVILIA: (*after looking off*) You will talk to him? About his letter. Why's he talking like this? Why did he send it to me? What's he going to do?

CICERO: Talk. You're right. That's all that letter is. He's— thinking. Trying to find a way to live. Not die. Otherwise, he— I'll speak with him.

SERVILIA: Thank you.

BRUTUS, *fishing pole in hand, enters,* PORCIA *just behind him.* CASSIUS, *also with pole, soon follows.*

BRUTUS: Mother.

SERVILIA: (*"smiling"*) I didn't mean to . . . Fish. Fish.

No response.

Cassius! You're here too.

BRUTUS: You didn't know Cassius was here? Where did you think he was?

SERVILIA: And my grandson? I was told you were all fishing.

No response.

> (*to* CASSIUS) I've heard from your wife. She thinks she'll be sent home soon. (*to* CICERO) The things we do for our children.

CICERO: Does Junia write about the war?

SERVILIA *nods.*

SERVILIA: She says it's been—brutal. No clemency. None. Heads on pikes. That sort of victory. Very unlike Caesar. You can tell she's been scared.

Another awkward moment.

CICERO: Sit. Sit. We'll get more stools— What else is a villa in the country good for—but sitting around and talking about—things?

SERVILIA: (*desperate, to* BRUTUS) How's the fishing?

BRUTUS: (*to* CICERO) Cassius was just saying that Antony's drunk half of the time now.

CASSIUS: He threw up in a theater.

BRUTUS: And now they're passing out a petition—to change the law—so Caesar can marry as often as he wants.

SERVILIA: I heard that too—

CICERO: (*at the same time*) What? Why?

BRUTUS: He's going to marry the Egyptian queen.

CICERO: My *god.*

BRUTUS: And move the capital— (*to* CASSIUS) Isn't that what you heard?

CASSIUS: She's visited him in Spain. She's pregnant again. Maybe she met my wife. (*short pause*) The fishing—it was just getting interesting. Just started to bite. That time of day. Excuse me. (*He turns to go.*)

SERVILIA: This has been hard for me as well. I am her mother.

PORCIA: Let the poor man go fish.

SERVILIA: Why are you saying that to me? I'm not the one who—

PORCIA: Leave him alone!

SERVILIA: What am I doing to him?!

PORCIA: What haven't you done?!

Pause. No one knows what to say after this confrontation.

CASSIUS: As I was saying—the fishing, it was just getting good. I'll go back to my son. Keep him company.

CICERO: (*looking off*) Here comes your son now.

CASSIUS: (*shouts off*) Stay there! I'm coming!

SERVILIA: Let me go and see my grandson—

She starts to move.

CASSIUS: (*shouts*) No!! No. Stay away from him. Please don't even look at him. I'm afraid you'll just turn him into stone. (*He hurries off.*)

Short pause.

SERVILIA: (*looking off*) He's gotten taller. Filling out. And handsome, don't you think?

CICERO: (*staring off as well, half to himself*) Such innocence. This is what I've lost. (*short pause; then to the others*) We can talk about real estate. That usually gets our mind off the world.

BRUTUS: He's understandably confused. He's trying to accept it.

SERVILIA: You can't just tell Caesar no.

BRUTUS: We know that. He knows that.

SERVILIA: What choice did I—?

BRUTUS: I'm not saying you did—have a choice.

PORCIA: (*to* BRUTUS) We disagree.

BRUTUS: (*to* PORCIA) She's my mother!

SERVILIA: Things will get better. They go in cycles. We just have to not panic.

BRUTUS: (*to* SERVILIA) Why are you here?

CICERO: She's here to sell Cato's property. She's here to—set a price?

SERVILIA *nods.*

And maybe—see if it's been attacked? Plundered. I've seen fires coming from over there.

SERVILIA: That too. (*pause*) We all grew up there. All of us. Even her (*indicating* PORCIA). One way or another. Cicero was telling me, he bought his property because—

PORCIA *turns away, looks off at the hillside.*

And now I have to sell it. (*She stands.*) I probably should take a look. Walk around Cato's property. See what's . . .

CICERO: Porcia, why don't you walk with her?

PORCIA: (*surprised*) What? Why?

CICERO: Go with her. She's not a young woman. And—talk among yourselves.

PORCIA *hesitates, then goes to* SERVILIA.

PORCIA: So—it's almost the end of "July." Isn't that what we're supposed to call it now? July? What else is he going to name after himself? The earth? The sky?

SERVILIA: I'm going ahead. She can catch up if she wants. (*She goes.*)

CICERO: (*to* PORCIA) Go. Go with her. I knew your father my whole life. That is his sister. Be nice. Come on. She shouldn't be alone.

PORCIA *looks to* BRUTUS, *who avoids her.*

Catch up to her. She won't bite.

She goes.

I don't think. (*smiles at* BRUTUS)

CICERO *and* BRUTUS *are alone now.*

I like your wife. I enjoy her visits. She's not sick of reading me yet. Did you know she wrote me the most extraordinary letter when Tullia died? I stole some of—it's in my book. There is something about her—she understands loss. Being sad. With some women it's just the way the eyelids— It looks— But Porcia understands. Doesn't she?

No response. CICERO *takes out the letter* SERVILIA *has given him and sets it on a stool next to him.* BRUTUS *watches this; looks at the letter without picking it up.*

(*"explaining"*) A letter your mother showed me. She got it this week, she said. (*changing the subject*) Let me show you something. (*takes out another book from his bag*) Seen this? He's written about Cato—

BRUTUS: I've read it.

CICERO: (*ignoring him*) Where does Caesar find the time? I thought he was fighting this war in Spain? (*opens the book, thumbs through*) Calls Cato a drunkard? A miser? Cato. A wild man whose death he describes as a beast tearing itself apart. Who is going to believe that? You can lie only so far—even him. People won't take it. (*short pause*) There'll be an uproar. Right? Righteous indignation will triumph! Right? (*short pause*) Maybe not. Maybe just a lot of stomachs grumbling. But I look at it as a very interesting development. Showing another side of Caesar. How sensitive he actually is. And therefore—vulnerable.

For the first time, BRUTUS *looks at him.*

It won't be long. He's pushing things way too far. People will say, enough is enough. Right? And we'll start to put our country back together. The way it should be. The way it's meant to be. The way you and I, Brutus, love it. Just a little more time. (*short pause*) Patience. We mustn't do anything foolish—to ourselves.

They look at each other.

There is much to learn from Cato—but not this. This wasn't his point. To kill ourselves. (*smiles*) Not that I haven't thought of it as well after my daughter— As you know. It was so tempting. I'd get letters from Rome—come back, we need help. I'd hear what was happening. I knew there was nothing I could do. There are times when we want to just cover our heads. I understand. But what Cato—what we should learn: this—that we carry around with us our own choices. We have choice. We are responsible. We can act. We are free. We are not at the will of the gods. Floating along on waves of fate. No "destiny." But what we are is what we choose to be. (*short pause*) Cato—by his death, by his death by his *own* hand—the lesson here is that we are free to decide for ourselves. Man is great. He—we are beautiful creatures—and we don't just throw that away.

BRUTUS: (*standing*) She shouldn't have shown you my letter.

CICERO: Sit down. Sit—down, Brutus.

He sits, then stands.

BRUTUS: I know everything you are going to say. And that's not to say I don't appreciate it.

CICERO: Sit down!!

He doesn't sit.

BRUTUS: The first—the first thing I think about in the morning— I don't sleep. But I start thinking—is peace. Not for the world. (*smiles*) God forbid. In here. (*points to his head*)

CICERO: Pain, grief, anger, mourning—these are acts of will. We can conquer them, my friend.

BRUTUS: I have held a knife up here (*points to his throat*) so many times. What stops me?

CICERO: I don't know.

BRUTUS: (*suddenly shouts*) No, you don't!! What stops me—is I see *his* face. And he is pleased. He knows he's killed me—with my own hands. So I don't let him do it. I take the knife away.

CICERO: One finds happiness—and you know this well, Brutus—not in the world but in oneself. One can find virtue, live a good life—here (*indicates Tusculum*), for example.

BRUTUS: Like you?

CICERO: I wasn't saying—I wouldn't hold myself up as—

BRUTUS: Porcia understands. When you've seen everything around you rot. Your world and country. I dream— (*looks at* CICERO) I dream of holding my knife at his throat.

CICERO: (*suddenly*) Stop that. Stop! That's madness. And then what—?

BRUTUS: Why madness?!

CICERO: There are others who will take his place.

BRUTUS: Are there?

CICERO: Antony.

BRUTUS: Antony's a fool. He's not Caesar.

CICERO: And what will happen after? Have you thought of that?

BRUTUS: It's him or me. And by the same hand.

CICERO: And we become like him? Animals? Slitting our Roman throats? What are we saving?

BRUTUS: Perhaps we're saving nothing. Maybe there's nothing left to save.

CICERO: How can you—?

BRUTUS: Maybe it's gone, old man!!

CICERO: We must do all to preserve the Republic. Even if it means—having a little patience, and in time . . .

BRUTUS: What if there's no Republic left? What if they destroy it while we're being patient? What if there's nothing left to preserve? What if while we sit here—they continue, as they have, inch by inch, brick by brick, to take apart everything? While we sit and read, and we write our books, put on our plays, make money, talk about real estate, fish—everything—gone. And we have nothing. There is nothing left. Worth living for!! (*short pause*) That's how I wake up in the morning. That's what I was feeling when I wrote my mother. I thought, I wondered, if she'd felt the same way, given . . . But now I see she doesn't . . . (*gestures to the letter*) Grief is not an act of will—that we can overcome, Cicero—at least not alone. Or by studying, writing . . . You kid yourself. (*short pause*) You can burn all the books in the world, destroy all the theaters, and you can still—have justice, liberty. Because that is between men and is done by action. But take away my country, you take away my soul, and then all the books, the plays, the conversations in places like here, in Tusculum— become just ways of passing the time. (*short pause*) It's you, Cicero, who by sitting here away from it all, you who are killing yourself. You who are the one preaching suicide—look at yourself. I'm trying to live and sur- vive. And if that means holding a knife to my throat or to his—

CICERO: (*stopping him*) We've never had this conversation. I want to know nothing more about it. Here. Take your let- ter back.

Hands it to BRUTUS, *who takes it.*

Pause.

(*suddenly erupts*) There is no one more outspoken against Caesar than me!!

BRUTUS: Where?!! In your garden?!! In your bath?!! So your words echo and sound almost full?!! Pretending you're in the Forum!

CICERO: I've criticized Caesar in the Forum!!

BRUTUS: When—was the last time?!! (*short pause*) Look at us. Look what we've become, and with us—everything we care about. He's found his way into us—how did he do that? How could we let him? There's talk that he's not done fighting yet. Spain isn't the end. We'll never stop. That's the kind of country we now find we live in. And you—write books . . . (*short pause*) Look at us. He forgave us. That forgiveness was the strongest leash he could ever have found. We are tethered to him. (*beat*) Look at us. This country was us. Our beliefs. Our ambitions. Our sense of right and wrong. What has happened to us? We were confident. Strong. How did he unravel that? How did he make us question what we know to be true? And right and good? How?!!!

SYRUS *has wandered in and heard the end of this. He stands at a distance and is about to leave when* BRUTUS *sees him.*

What's he doing here?

CICERO: He's my houseguest.

SYRUS: (*hesitates, then "smiles"*) Cicero's been very generous— Did I interrupt—? I can go back—

CICERO: No. Join us. Sit down.

SYRUS *sits, though is uncomfortable.*

SYRUS: (*"explaining" to* BRUTUS) I'm staying with Licinius next week. He's just—

BRUTUS: I know the villa.

SYRUS: Amazing library of books he has.

BRUTUS: I know about that too. But who needs more books? (*smiles*) I could live to five hundred and never read the books in his (*gesturing to* CICERO) house.

CICERO: And that's just counting the ones I've written.

He laughs. SYRUS *laughs.* BRUTUS *doesn't.*

BRUTUS: I'll get out of your hair. Thank you for the conversation.

BRUTUS *goes.*

SYRUS: Did I—?

CICERO: Yes. And no.

Pause. CICERO *is lost in thought.*

SYRUS: I ran into Cassius on my walk. He seems to have lost a lot of weight.

No response.

Nice man, Cassius. Very generous when he let me stay . . . (*new thought*) The thing about Licinius's library is—you close the shutters—just so there're those slices of light, through the— Pick a book. Best place in the world to sleep! (*laughs*) You forget everything!

CICERO *smiles. He is hardly listening.*

I saw Servilia. That was a surprise. She's selling Cato's villa for how much, did she tell you?

CICERO *shakes his head.*

Licinius was telling me last night that he'd been offered a fortune for his. From some rich Roman. Three times what he paid for it only a few years ago. (*short pause*) Where do people get the money? Where do they come from?

Scene 5

A month later; August. Morning. A room in CASSIUS *'s villa, Tusculum.*

CASSIUS *and* BRUTUS *enter, talking.*

BRUTUS: First, he's not well.

CASSIUS: What do you mean?

BRUTUS: He's frail. The war in Spain took a lot out of him, I think. He was very happy to see me. That I'd come.

CASSIUS: I'm sure—

BRUTUS: Just pushed a couple of people aside when he saw me. He's having headaches. And fits. More and more fits. One while I was there. He just . . . Everyone seems to be used to them. Kept on talking. (*shrugs*) His Egyptian whore just—like nothing was happening. Kept playing with her son.

CASSIUS: She's there?

BRUTUS: Like she's stuck to him.

CASSIUS: Where was this?

BRUTUS: He's stopped down the coast. Made camp there. He's waiting—for something. Before entering Rome. For it to feel right, I guess.

CASSIUS: For the excitement to build. He's a showman. Never forget that. Why didn't you come to me?

BRUTUS: I didn't have time. The messenger came in the middle—

CASSIUS: This wasn't safe.

BRUTUS: In the middle of the night. If I was going to come, I had to come with him. There was no time. What did I have to lose?

CASSIUS: Where do you want me to begin?

BRUTUS: What does that—?

PORCIA, *who has come to* CASSIUS*'s with* BRUTUS, *enters and stays at a distance. Both notice her now.*

  If you're saying he was using me—of course. I'm not an idiot, Cassius. I understood that. But don't we need to at least listen to what he says? If for no other reason than then we'll be prepared?

CASSIUS: With the knife to cut our throats? (*short pause*) Some things you shouldn't tell your friends. Forgive me, Brutus. I'm pleased you've gotten over that. Now—you're Caesar's friend.

BRUTUS: That's not fair.

CASSIUS: He pulls your chain and you run to him in the middle of the night! You're either his friend or his— (*gestures like he's yanking a leash*)

Pause.

He glances at PORCIA.

　　Does she have to stand there?

BRUTUS *waves* PORCIA *away. She goes off.*

BRUTUS: She and my mother have done nothing but fight. Since I've got back—she's just stared at me.

CASSIUS: Your mother knows you—?

BRUTUS: She said she'd been hoping for it. I take it that she's been talking with Caesar.

CASSIUS: Sit down. Sit down.

They sit.

　　What else? Talk to me.

BRUTUS: "No more war." The first words he said to me. It's been god-awful. Like he's been a sponge and now is full and can't take any more. That's what he said. We went for a walk around his camp. Then down by the shore. Along the beach. Just the two of us, Cassius. Him and me. (*short pause*) "What do I think? What's going on?" He kept asking me. Interested in everything I said. And I was honest. Then— (*He looks over his shoulder to be sure* PORCIA *is gone.*) "I forgive you," he says, "for marrying Cato's daughter." And then he slapped me on the back, and laughing, said, "But you don't need my forgiveness." (*He looks to* CASSIUS.) I told myself—he's using you, Brutus. Careful. But—I wasn't sure how. He honestly, genuinely seemed interested in what I had to say. Maybe this is all he wanted from me—to hear the truth. "There is no greater Roman"—he said this—"than Cato." His words.

CASSIUS *laughs.*

Why is that funny?

CASSIUS: The petitions are already going around—to make him Dictator for Life.

BRUTUS: I know that.

CASSIUS: A special seat is being built for him, as we speak, in the Forum. A golden throne in the Senate. A chariot and litter for his *statue* to be carried with those of the gods at the procession in the Circus!

BRUTUS: I know this. I know. I hear the gossip! But—what if he could be persuaded? He seems to have no one around him whom he trusts. And we know—he's getting very bad advice. It's frightening who's got their claws into him—

CASSIUS: I know that.

BRUTUS: I came away, convinced—that he needs us. People like us. And that he knows it. It's not that he's suddenly become someone else, I'm not saying— I'm not that naïve. But that he's made a very calculated decision. We could be a part of that. This—Dictator for Life, the other—I don't think it's going to happen. He's not pushing. He doesn't need that. (*pause*) Two days ago I wanted to kill him. Now I realize it's not him I want to kill. I think I was wrong. He's an old man, Cassius. Older than what we remember. And not well. We can have a significant influence. We can do something.

CASSIUS *stands and walks and thinks.*

Even my mother he doesn't see now—he is that cut off. (*short pause*) He spoke warmly of you, Cassius.

CASSIUS *turns and looks at* BRUTUS.

When I told him you were here. We were in Tusculum together. As a soldier. A leader. There's so much he says he wants to talk to you about. He said he's seen the barbarism—it was worse in Spain than anytime in Gaul. And that you'd understand that. He seemed scared. He'd seen what could happen to a civilization. He wants to talk to you.

CASSIUS: While he fucks my wife.

Short pause.

BRUTUS: Junia's back in Rome. We all do stupid— Out of— pride. Or—power. Politics is nasty. I think he couldn't break you—so your wife. We've talked about this. You understand this. She's now back in Rome. (*short pause*) I know—I hear myself too. I can't believe this is me. Yes— I felt flattered. Yes—I knew he was flattering me. Yes—I know he was after something from me. Do I sound desperate? You'd tell me if I did? Should I not have gone? (*short pause*) He said to ask you about Syria.

CASSIUS *stops.*

He said you'd know what he meant.

CASSIUS: Why bring that up?

BRUTUS: This was when you were with Crassus? You've never wanted to talk about that. You must have had some conversation with Caesar . . . There must be something he wants you to think about.

CASSIUS *doesn't say anything.*

He had welts on his arms from the flies in Spain. He showed me. He said you couldn't believe the flies. The cruelty of this war. The utter savagery. He said he'd accept no blame for the way his army behaved. Who's blaming—?

CASSIUS: I haven't heard—

BRUTUS: Me neither. They did, he said, only what they had to, to respond. The fault lay with the enemy. The gods gave him this duty to protect us, he hadn't wanted it. And if all the blood that's been spilled—he said there are heads on pikes as far as one can see, down one road. Corpses crushed and used as building materials. If this isn't enough to satisfy—if we Romans don't appreciate . . . And come together. He said that. What could he do? We sat on a rock, looking out at the sea. He'd been dragged by others, he said, into the bloody mud, it's not where he wanted to be. (*pause*) I don't know what I believe. I could go either way. I asked him if he believed in the Republic.

CASSIUS *is interested in this.*

He said—he did. Now either that is the truth and I live in hope. Or a lie, and in utter despair. If I give myself the choice . . . (*short pause*) A man overwhelmed by what he'd witnessed. In need of rest and peace. He told me—he'd written out his will. What about Syria? What did he mean?

Pause.

CASSIUS: Crassus was a terrible soldier, everyone now knows that. We were outmanned, outmaneuvered, outfought by these—Syrians. (*short pause*) But there was something different here. It wasn't army against army. Something else opened up, Brutus. They attacked, but they didn't have drums but some other sound that got in your head, in your stomach, and made you sick. Made it so you couldn't think. When they captured Crassus's son—they beheaded him on the hill in front of us. One of them, he pulled out most of what was inside, and sort of jammed a hand into the skull, fingers through the eyeholes, thumb out the mouth, tongue was still there. And he rode by us, arm up, like a puppet, pretending to give us orders. It was the first real hint that these "people" weren't just out to kill us, de-feat an army, but—to show contempt and hatred for a whole civilization. I'd never seen that before. (*short pause*) Crassus was captured. And first they picked an imperson-ator to pretend to be Crassus, dressed him as a woman, and marched him around with pretend "Senators," and "Romans," with "moneybags" hanging off of us. Their whores singing beside "us" as if they were our women. (*short pause*) Crassus was butchered in sight of us, those left. And his head, after feeding his brains to the dogs, it's been reported, was sent to a local theater performance where it was used to publicly drink from and piss in. (*short pause*) There are people out there who hate us. This was when I saw this. Probably trying to flatter Caesar, I told him this. And told him that it's people like him, or maybe just him, who stand between all of us and that bloody barbarian horde. (*short pause*) No doubt, that's what he wanted me to remember. (*pause*) It's why, Brutus, I haven't known what to do. Because no matter how dis-gusted or angry or personally hurt I become—it always comes back to: if we lose Caesar—do we lose everything else?

Pause.

BRUTUS: Then I think we agree. We make a mistake sitting here in our villas on a hill—looking down. There is room for us. It's not over.

CASSIUS: No.

BRUTUS: We may not end up with the Republic of our dreams, but it will still have its essence. And soul.

CASSIUS: I agree.

BRUTUS: He really didn't seem like a man itching to rule us. It's those hangers-on. They're after anything, hands out, manipulating. (*smiles and hits* CASSIUS *on the shoulder*) You should have seen the faces when he took me by the shoulder and we walked—*alone*—he made that clear with just a gesture— (*makes a dismissive gesture*) —down to that beach.

They laugh.

CASSIUS: Cleopatra's a terrible influence.

BRUTUS: She is.

CASSIUS: She cares nothing for laws. She knows nothing about them.

BRUTUS: She raced to him. I'm told, as soon as he landed.

CASSIUS: That's one thing we'll have to do—pull them apart.

BRUTUS: One thing he did ask.

CASSIUS: What's that?

BRUTUS: He said—listen to this. I quote: "It is better to extend the frontiers of the mind, than to push back the boundaries of the empire." He meant—Cicero. He said that was how he felt about Cicero. He wants him to write him. To ask to meet.

CASSIUS: Why doesn't Caesar write him?

BRUTUS: Must feel he can't. (*shrugs*) Maybe there have been words. Things written. (*then new subject*) Cassius, the reason he pardoned us? It wasn't to humiliate. When I said this—

CASSIUS: You talked about—?

BRUTUS: Yes! Not to humiliate but to—he knew he'd need our help sometime—our ideas. Once all this—the war. Now! I said you'd felt the same way. So I'd tell you.

CASSIUS *looks at him, a little confused, then another slap on the shoulder from* BRUTUS.

> The two of us on that beach—we wanted to talk about farming! He wants to farm! Grow things! I said I did too! (*another thought*) He no longer drinks.

BRUTUS *gets up. He is about to go.*

CASSIUS: You think Cicero will write to Caesar? He won't see that as groveling?

BRUTUS: How is it groveling? He's writing to advise. To explain what he thinks Caesar should do. Give him a direction. Fight over his soul. How can Cicero say no to that?

They head off.

Scene 6

The same morning, an hour or so later. A room in CICERO's *villa. Only one candle is lit, the rest of the room is dark. The shutters are closed; slivers of sunlight cut through the shutter slats.*

CICERO *sits, holding a lap desk.* BRUTUS *enters.*

BRUTUS: Is this where you sleep?

CICERO: I don't sleep.

BRUTUS: Should I open the shutters? It's morning. It's been morning.

CICERO: No.

Pause.

Dogs bark off.

BRUTUS: I'll open one.

He opens a shutter. PORCIA *is revealed standing in a corner of the room.*

What are you doing here?

CICERO: We've been reminiscing about her father. That man had no sense of humor. Did he?

PORCIA: (*looking at* BRUTUS) No.

CICERO: I remember when there was snow. First time I'd seen snow. I was here visiting Cato. He was home from school. He told me it was the clouds falling down. That's the only time I ever heard him even try and make a joke. And he wasn't trying to make a joke, he was trying to—in the end—make me feel stupid. Which he always did. (*pause*) He was the worst judge of art. The things he liked . . . That man—he lived in his head. You think I'm— He didn't care what he wore. He walked around barefoot sometimes. He'd just forget to wear . . . (*to* PORCIA) Isn't that right?

PORCIA: He would. I remember that.

CICERO *looks to* BRUTUS, *who is staring at his wife.*

CICERO: He drank like a fish. That's when you didn't want to argue with him.

PORCIA: No.

CICERO: She knows. But then you knew him well. I know how much you admired him. That man didn't know how to compromise.

BRUTUS: (*to* PORCIA) What have you been doing here?

CICERO: (*to* PORCIA) I think you should go.

She nods and leaves.

Pause.

She says your mother has been treating her very badly.

BRUTUS: Is that why she's here? To complain about my mother?

CICERO: When your mother visited, she complained about her. (*smiles*) Everyone talks to me. They think I have— wisdom. What does that mean?

BRUTUS: My wife, you have to understand, is like one of the peasants in the south—you insult one of their family— they never forget. Vengeance. They live on it.

CICERO: Oh. One of those—with loyalty.

BRUTUS *looks at him.*

(*trying to be light*) I asked if she has any money to loan me. She doesn't. (*He smiles.*)

No response from BRUTUS.

(*suddenly serious*) That woman would be able to slit her own throat. Which is more than you can say for the rest of us. As I'm learning. You're a lucky husband.

BRUTUS: What did she—?

CICERO: (*interrupting*) Let me read you something. What I've been up all night writing. (*reads from his papers*)

"Nature—not content to give us bodies that are weak, susceptible to illness and disease and unendurable agonies, has also given us hearts and souls just as weak, also susceptible to such agonies as well as those heartbreaks that are just their own." (*short pause*) "But maybe I have got it all wrong, when looking for goodness in only the absence of bad. Perhaps if goodness does indeed exist in man—and who, Brutus, more than your uncle, Cato, proves—"

BRUTUS: To—?

CICERO: Shh. (*continuing*) "—proves that to be true—it is a thing of its own with its own qualities and attributes. And we, human beings, may again and again fail to attain this standard of goodness, because we are afraid, scared, or simply deficient—it does not mean we give up this effort. Trying to be good, and do good is in itself a worthwhile human pursuit."

He sets his lap desk and his papers on the floor.

BRUTUS: To me? You're writing this to me?

CICERO: When I'm thinking, I always pretend I'm speaking *to* someone. Recently, it's been you. When it hasn't been Tullia. This was her room. She died in here. I've made it mine—where I think. Where I don't forget.

Long pause.

BRUTUS: (*as he sits*) Did Porcia tell—?

CICERO: Yes. I know where you've been. Who you've been with. (*short pause*) I heard as soon as you'd been summoned. I've imagined what has happened. And I've now heard, from your wife, what you want from me.

BRUTUS: (*hesitates*) I will just say, then, what's on my mind and be done with it. I believe this is a great country.

CICERO *looks at him.*

I know you do too. Worth saving. Worth trying almost anything to—

CICERO: There we disagree—

BRUTUS: I have written him. Cassius and I. Asking to see him again. Before he goes to Rome. We think we can have influence. After being with him alone—did she tell you we were alone—?

CICERO: What does that—?

BRUTUS: More than anything else I felt—

CICERO: You've just met with him.

BRUTUS: Yesterday, *he* sent for me. This time—*we* initiate—

CICERO: What difference does that—?

BRUTUS: Stop this. Write him the damn letter! Ask to see him! Do something! That's what we're doing. Stop writing "the truth" and start writing to change things!

CICERO: You're throwing everything you've ever believed—

BRUTUS: (*over this*) Stop writing about "goodness" and start doing some good!!

CICERO: Is that a campaign saying now? Is that how you're now talking—? Did Caesar give you that to say?

BRUTUS: I'm talking about recognizing that perhaps we can have a little more influence over events—what Caesar does—over the future of our nation—than we've thought. How much did she tell you about my visit with—?

CICERO: (*turning away*) I heard all about it.

BRUTUS: I love this country. Do you?

CICERO: That's unfair. That's unthinking—

BRUTUS: To love one's country?

CICERO: To talk like that.

BRUTUS: He's surrounded by bad people, I think he knows that now. He has reached out a hand; he wants us there—a place at the table. Why shouldn't we take it? Which we can do, we need only the smallest possible compromise. If that's even what it is. A gesture. (*short pause*) Perhaps we have been too proud? Perhaps we need to get over our pride and realize this is not about ourselves? How we see ourselves? How we've been hurt, things that have been said, what's been done to us? We must be bigger than that. Let us wade into the shit. As long as we keep it below our waist, we're not going to drown. We are statesmen. We belong there at that table. (*short pause*) He's a very tired man.

Finished with war. There's nothing left to conquer and the last one scared him. You see that. I have. It is time the Republic was supported again. This glorious and great Republic for which we've all bled, for which we'd gladly give our lives. You too, I know this. (*short pause*) Mind if I open another shutter? I can hardly see your face.

Opens a shutter; bright light pours in. CICERO *covers his eyes at first.*

(*at the window*) I love these hills as much as you do. My whole childhood was here. But we must—grow up.

CICERO: (*erupts*) I've been grown up!! I've served this nation. I've written its laws! I've stood day after day on the floor of the Senate—arguing for this nation. Fighting to keep it alive. Now—I don't see it. I want to, Brutus. Believe me. I so want to . . . (*short pause*) A few weeks ago you—

BRUTUS: That was before—

CICERO: (*over this*) I look at you and see this sudden belief? Hope?? Where did it spring from?

BRUTUS: I told you—

CICERO: I mean—from what well? What well hadn't dried up? I know of none in me with anything left. I look at you and see this— Coming from—wherever. You were a man in despair.

BRUTUS: I know.

CICERO: And now— I think maybe you're right. Maybe it is our only chance—you extinguish hope, belief that your country— And then what is there left to life? But sitting alone—shutters closed . . . (*short pause*) I love this nation too.

BRUTUS: I—

CICERO: The pride in knowing we live in a republic, where there is justice and a respect for the human mind. I have stood in Rome and listened astounded at the spoken ideals that sew us together as a people. Where barbarism is everywhere, here we can bask in the glow of the gods. If all is just raw power—if there is nothing deeper to define us as human—what are we? What do we become? (*short pause*) I do love this *country*. I do love its people. I love what we've built and created. I love what was once its great messy optimism, its blind hope and sense of being invulnerable . . . Its sense of justice. Fairness. Of trying to do good. None of this, Brutus, do I see anymore. Except perhaps now—the slight glow that I see around you . . .

BRUTUS: Don't give up.

CICERO: (*shouts*) It's not me who has given up on my country, it's my country that has given up on me! (*pause*) Tell me, because I'd like to know, maybe learn—how does someone (*gestures to* BRUTUS) despair so one day, then just like that—

BRUTUS: Because I believe that the world can change. It doesn't have to be as it is. That's what I've found.

CICERO: I want to find that too. I want to feel strongly one day, then totally different the next. I want to be young. (*He smiles.*) And fickle. And irresponsible. (*stares at* BRUTUS) When are you asking to see Caesar?

BRUTUS: As soon as he'll see us.

Short pause.

CICERO: I won't write to ask to be seen by him. There are things I cannot do. But—I will write something that you and Cassius can take along with you. I'll—praise some of his recent writing. (*makes a strangling gesture*) As much as that pains me. But as you say—not everything in life need be the truth. And he'll understand the gesture. Caesar is good at understanding gestures. We'll see what he says.

BRUTUS: Thank you. A greeting from Cicero to Caesar will make a great difference, I'm sure. He'll see we are a bigger, more united force than his advisers think. He can't ignore us. He can't—not listen.

CICERO *smiles.*

Why are you smiling?

CICERO *begins to write the note.*

CICERO: (*as he writes*) If only we were more like our ancestors, Brutus. Those men were gods. They fought for ideals. To change how men think about themselves. We fight for a seat at a table. To talk. When it's our turn. To argue to keep a little of what we've already got. We've become very small. I mean—me.

Finishes the note, hands it to BRUTUS.

I praise his writing style in his last book. I call it concise and to the point. In fact, it's confused and sloppy. He'll save this and show it around.

BRUTUS: Thank you.

CICERO: A small gesture. Unlike Cassius. I don't think I could forget all he's forgetting.

BRUTUS: He knows he can't let his private life interfere with his duty to his country.

CICERO: No. We can't allow that.

BRUTUS *starts to go, stops.*

BRUTUS: Would you like these (*indicating the shutters*) closed?

CICERO *shakes his head.*

CICERO: Once the world's in, you can't get it out . . . (*then stopping* BRUTUS) Brutus . . .

BRUTUS *turns back.*

There is much that can be done in a room—like this. Much good.

BRUTUS: I wasn't saying—

CICERO: An assistant of mine has compiled a list. (*He looks among his papers.*) Here it is. A list—of words. Words.

That *I* have put into our language. Words that did not exist. Words I have—invented? So we could understand the great Greeks. All civilization comes from them, you know this.

BRUTUS: Of course.

CICERO: Sometimes culture must stand at a distance from— Because they don't understand. Anyway, the list. Of words we didn't have and now do. Do you mind?

BRUTUS: Please.

CICERO: (*reads the list*) "Element. Quality. Vacuum. Moral. Individual. Definition. Induction. Property. Infinity. Comprehension. Appetite. Instance. Image. Difference. Notion. Science. Species . . ." (*pause*) I read this over and I was amazed. I hadn't realized. I don't mean in a proud way. You don't realize all we *didn't* know. All we didn't have words for. How many more words will we need? How much more is there to know, to try and say? (*short pause*) We can love our country and our countrymen—in different ways. Doing different things.

BRUTUS: We'll come and see you as soon as we're back.

CICERO: I shall keep a candle lit in the window.

BRUTUS *goes.*

Pause.

CICERO *goes back to his writing. After a while he looks up.*

Tullia, dear daughter—my inspiration. What do you think? You're young. And I'm old. (*Shakes his head, goes back to writing.*) Tullia, tell me what you think of this. (*He reads.*) "Anyone who fears pain or death must inevitably be unhappy. Because pain is frequent and death always hovers nearby. Anyone who is afraid of poverty, disgrace, scandal, terrified of bodily collapse, blindness, slavery—a disaster which often overtakes not just individuals but entire communities—he surely can't possibly be happy. There are those who aren't just worried but have actually suffered such onslaughts, add to the list exile, bereavement, and inexpressible grief at the loss of a child . . ." (*He pauses for a moment.*) "Who of these can be happy? The man driven to a mad frenzy by lust, or the person who lets frivolities completely dominate him, such a man may think he's happy, but the more he tries to convince himself of this, the more desperately miserable his existence really is." (*Short pause. He writes the conclusion.*) "So to find happiness, at first we'll need to conquer our fears. But who today—isn't afraid?"

Scene 7

The following week. It is still August. Afternoon. The hills near Brutus's villa, Tusculum.

CASSIUS *sits alone on a bench, lost in thought.* CICERO *appears in the distance and slowly approaches.* CASSIUS *turns when he hears* CICERO *approaching.*

CICERO: (*after a pause*) I just heard you were back. I thought someone was going to come and get me. Tell me. I've been waiting.

No response.

When did you return?

CASSIUS: This morning. A while ago. (*short pause*) Brutus is fishing. I haven't been to my home yet either. My wife's there.

CICERO: I know. (*to say something*) It's hot today. Hardly a breeze. Typical summer's day. It's hard to sleep. In this heat. (*short pause*) I saw your wife—while you were away. She and Porcia came for a visit. She hadn't seen my villa for ages, she said. I showed her my sculpture. She loved my Hermathena. She has good taste.

No response.

We sat outside and talked about gardens.

CASSIUS: Did you.

CICERO: She—knows gardens. She was able to help—point out what was what. She really knows her—

CASSIUS: She's from here. She grew up here. So that's not surprising. That she knows the plants.

CICERO: Of course.

They look off at the hills.

She said—her hope was to get "lost" in her garden. It's good she's in the country. Should we get Brutus? If he's only fishing . . .

CASSIUS: He knows you're here. We both saw you coming.

CICERO: And he went fishing? (*pause*) How long were you—there?

CASSIUS: Three whole days.

CICERO: Did he make you wait, or did he see you at once?

CASSIUS: At once.

CICERO: And he wasn't surprised?

CASSIUS: He was. He tried not to show it at first—but he was. And—intrigued.

CICERO: I'm—

CASSIUS: Why were we there? Initially—he stopped everything—to meet with us. You should have seen the face of those— The ones around. Even his Egyptian, she, you could tell, was trying to stay back and listen to what . . . But—"Out!" Everyone out. He wanted to "spend some time with his friends." Me and . . . (*short pause*) It was more than we'd expected, actually. But it fit. What Brutus had been saying how Caesar— There was no one for him to talk to. So . . . He could not have been more interested. Brutus was very good. Very—generous. We presented our case. For the Republic. Our rights. The importance of the Senate as a true governing body, not just something to be—to just say yes. To respect that and other opinions. To listen. Like he was so generously doing right then, Brutus said. (*short pause*) He asked questions. Who felt this way. Who didn't.

CICERO: You didn't tell him.

CASSIUS: No. No. We weren't idiots. We wouldn't give him names. Just us. We were only speaking for us.

CICERO: Good.

CASSIUS *stands, looks off at the hills.*

CASSIUS: Brutus gave him a brief history of the Republic.

CICERO: I'll bet he liked that.

CASSIUS: Of course he knew—

CICERO: But he listened?

CASSIUS: He tried. He got distracted.

CICERO: He doesn't—

CASSIUS: He doesn't "focus" for very—

CICERO: No, he doesn't. We all know this.

CASSIUS: Two, three times, various "advisers" tried to barge in, obviously they were very very curious—

CICERO: Very worried.

CASSIUS: Yes. But he just wanted us. For—it must have been three, four hours.

CICERO: Was he drinking?

CASSIUS: No. He doesn't anymore. We asked around . . . Nothing. Nor does he sit still for very long. He moves— Like he can't sit still.

CICERO: It was better when he was drinking.

CASSIUS: Was it? (*short pause*) He let us talk. Then when he felt we'd said our peace, and we pretty much had—at least enough to get an honest conversation going, he asks— actually the first thing he does ask us: he wonders if we'd support a resolution, a petition, declaring—

CICERO: Him Dictator for Life. We know all about this.

CASSIUS: No. Declaring him Divus Julius. Julius, the god. I thought he was joking. Maybe just seeing how we'd react. Brutus first smiled, then . . . Well, Caesar dropped it. No more mention of that. He, uh—started to detail his plans. All he wants to do. (*looks at* CICERO) And he has this question—were we, the Roman people, the Republic, capable of working with him? Would we see the virtues of all he needs—"needs" was the word—to accomplish? And soon. Could we do that? Or were we just talk? Were we just something that was in the way, something there just to slow him down?

Short pause.

CICERO: What does he want to do? Need to do?

CASSIUS: Quite impressive, really. The list—Brutus took notes. Let me see. He is sending veterans into the provinces, granting them full Roman citizenship and the right to grant the same to others. He says—he wants to make the world—Rome.

CICERO: What does that mean?

CASSIUS: We weren't sure. And then—he moves on. To how he wishes to rebuild Carthage and Corinth—as monuments to this new age of peace. Carthage, he insists, must forever put Utica in its shade—and those what are still bitter memories of Cato and his—and these are Caesar's exact words—cowardly death. Cato—by the way—that brought a tangent that lasted an hour. He is very spooked by that man.

CICERO: Good.

Pause.

CASSIUS: By the way, it's extraordinary how much he follows—about Cato's villa here. What it's worth. What it might be sold for. Who might purchase it. Servilia obviously keeps him well informed.

CICERO: She would. We all know that.

CASSIUS: Maybe.

CICERO: Doesn't Brutus—?

CASSIUS: I don't think he does. I don't think he's thought about— He's younger sometimes than we think. (*short pause*) So—build a world out of these ashes of war. Rome too. He has big plans for Rome. A new theater, bigger than Pompey's. The biggest temple in the world. A library. And—he has decided to divert the course of the Tiber. He doesn't like how it—something. I don't know. It is like he's a god, pointing his finger there, and there, and there. Brutus and I were impressed. And he could see that. I'm not sure he'd shared the full scope of it all with anyone before. We were maybe his first audience. He insisted that we stay the night. What could we say? As we were about to leave him, he looked back and forth at both of us and said—I have no plans to abolish the Republic.

CICERO: Really? He said that.

CASSIUS: Why, he said, why destroy what is nothing and no longer exists? (*short pause*) Then suddenly others came in,

I don't know how they knew, and we were swept up. Each in a different direction. Each with a flock of—people wanting something. Being with Caesar, alone with him for that length of time—everyone knew that it meant we had power or influence or . . . I don't know. Something. People wanting work. Attention for their projects. Claims. Others just wanting to know us, in case it would help them with some unspecified thing later. We didn't see each other until later that night.

BRUTUS *appears in the distance. First* CICERO, *then* CASSIUS *notices this.*

As soon as we were back together—one of Caesar's I don't know—I didn't know him—he wants to see me. Alone. Brutus, I can tell, thinks I should go. See what this is about. So I go. And this—lackey—he says Caesar wants to know if I'd accept an "appointment" as Chief Administrator for Central Rome.

CICERO: My god.

CASSIUS: That's what I thought. I was being leapfrogged over I don't know how many others. Picking me out of the blue. For *god's* sake, I'd fought with Pompey against him! I was flattered.

CICERO: The point.

CASSIUS: I suppose. Yes. Partially. I accepted. What could I do?

CICERO: Is that a question?

CASSIUS: No. I went back to the tent. I didn't know how I was going to tell Brutus. So—I didn't tell him anything. But then he didn't ask me, did he?

CICERO: He didn't want to know—?

BRUTUS *has been listening and getting closer to them.*

BRUTUS: In the meantime—

CICERO *is startled and turns to* BRUTUS.

—at the same time, another of these flunkeys, while Cassius was . . . He was meeting with me. And he was asking if I'd accept an appointment: Chief Administrator of all of Rome.

CICERO: (*to* CASSIUS) Your boss.

CASSIUS: Yes. That's right.

CICERO *smiles. He is now figuring things out.*

So we both have news, but don't know how to—

CICERO: (*to* BRUTUS) You accepted?

CASSIUS: He did. (*short pause*) How to tell each other. What to tell each other.

CICERO: That in itself should have made you both question—

BRUTUS: It did!

Short pause.

CASSIUS: We know there are people outside the tent—

CICERO: Spies.

CASSIUS: No doubt told to find out if we tell each other.

CICERO: He was having fun with you. (*laughs to himself*)

BRUTUS: Yes.

CICERO: How did you—? Who told the other—?

BRUTUS: Neither. We don't tell each other. We don't find out for two whole days. We'd made our own deals. We'd cut each other out.

CASSIUS: That's not how we saw it. By accepting the position, we'd be able in the future to help—

BRUTUS: We cut each other out.

CICERO: Oh, he enjoyed that.

BRUTUS: I'm sure.

CASSIUS: For two days, neither of us sleeps. Looking for that chance to tell the other. (*to* BRUTUS) At least I was. That's what we were doing, wasn't it?

BRUTUS: I don't know.

CASSIUS: (*to* CICERO) Of course it just got harder. And—it's extraordinary when you are seen as—well, under his wing, his arm, how you are treated.

BRUTUS: Like gods.

CASSIUS: I suppose. That's true. By dawn he is asking for us again.

BRUTUS: He doesn't sleep. Says he can't anymore. We're told he wants to go over his plans with us. I'm thinking—we're going to see where he wants to divert the Tiber. More grandiose visions for Rome. This building craze that he has for monuments to himself. But he doesn't talk about any of this. It's like he's given up on all that. In just one night. Got bored? And now—talks only of war.

CICERO: What war??

BRUTUS: Syria. That appears to be next on his list.

CASSIUS: The excuse? To avenge Crassus. That idiot. I was there.

CICERO: I knew you were—

BRUTUS: Ten years ago that happened. He was just looking for an excuse—

CICERO: He has never mentioned—

BRUTUS: Probably just thought of it. Sixteen legions.

CICERO: No.

BRUTUS: He leaves again in the spring. He'll be gone at least three years. (*short pause*) He gives us nothing—to fight against. He makes it so we can't fight him.

CICERO: Of course.

CASSIUS: War, he says—now we're not alone. You can see that he's brought others there to watch our reaction. How we react to this "news." That will be how Rome reacts. That is what he is thinking. That is what he has told them, I'm sure. (*short pause*) War, he says—it's best for Rome. We need a war—to keep us focused. And he gestures to himself and his cronies. And—to keep them—gestures to us—scared. (*short pause*) Hard to value words too much when you've sixteen legions training and trained. Important to remind people like them—me, him—how little of what they have they can keep without us.

BRUTUS: "What about all the changes? The monuments? The theaters?" we ask. He looks confused. "Everything you told us yesterday?" (*short pause*) "Once the wars are over. Once there is peace." Perpetual war—that is his philosophy.

Silence.

CASSIUS: When he got up and all the others got up, and as we were leaving his tent, he turns to me—Cassius, I hear you've accepted the position. (*short pause*) "What position?" Brutus asks. Didn't you hear, says Caesar—and he announces that I'm the new Chief Administrator for Central Rome. I look at Brutus, who is in shock. "I guess he didn't tell his friend," cries Caesar. Big smile on his face. Of course he already knew that, he had the spies. And everyone's laughing. "So I guess, Brutus, you didn't tell your friend your news either." Now the laughing is deafening. (*Short pause. He looks at* BRUTUS.) And we look at each other, don't we? We know we've been used.

CICERO: Why did you accept?

CASSIUS: (*after a glance at* BRUTUS) Because I thought it'd help. A foot in the door. Change things.

CICERO: Then why keep it from each other?

No response. CASSIUS *continues with his story.*

CASSIUS: We walk through the camp and don't say anything. We're no longer in a big tent, near Caesar's, we're on the edge of the camp now, tiny little place, mud. You hear people laugh as they go by. We don't speak to each other for the rest of the night.

Short pause.

BRUTUS: Except—

CASSIUS: Except for a minute or two. One of us pushes the other, we start shoving and shouting at each other like eight-year-old boys. We literally start hitting each other, or trying to, with our fists. It was pathetic.

BRUTUS: Yes.

CASSIUS: He's brought us that low. That quickly. And then we came home. This is the most we've talked.

PORCIA *has appeared in the distance.*

PORCIA: (*calls*) Cassius, your wife's here. She's heard—you are back.

Short pause.

CASSIUS: (*to* CICERO) And that is it. I'm sorry I went. Excuse me. (*starts to go, stops*) He's had my wife, now he's had me. I suppose that gives us something to talk about.

CASSIUS *goes.* PORCIA *starts to follow.*

BRUTUS: You can stay if you wish.

She stays at a distance and listens.

CICERO: Well—at least now we know that it's not just all the bad people around him. We've learned that. (*He starts to stand.*)

BRUTUS: I gave him your letter. Note.

CICERO *sits back down.*

He asked to see me a third time, to talk about it. Cassius doesn't know this. They came and got me while he was asleep. (*short pause*) There was a crowd. They were expecting me. Obviously he'd read the letter out loud more than once already. He has it in his hand. He wants me to hear it. He wants to see my face, Cicero. (*short pause*) I'll spare you the specifics.

CICERO *shrugs.*

Let's just say—he hates, detests everything you and I stand for. He says—and look at this praise this great writer, Cicero, gives me! Lavishing upon me. And for what? You think I don't know it's crap? But the point is—I got *him* to praise crap. So whose words matter more? (*short pause*) I'm sorry. I tried to defend you. To explain—

CICERO: That was stupid.

BRUTUS: I know. So what do you believe? he asks me. "Is this good writing or not? I think it's crap what I've written, do you agree or disagree?" (*short pause*) I avoid the question. I say on the one hand, on the other— And then he goes for me. "You people," he says. "The problem with you people is that you think too much. You think about it this way, then another way—until you don't know which way. Until you don't know what to do except talk some more about it. That is what makes you weak. You think too much. You talk too much. You try to understand things. Look at our friend Cicero . . ." (*short pause*) "He sits alone in his villa in this Tusculum—I know where he is, people tell me where he is—writing book after book. *A Life of Study.* What does that mean? Why does that matter? Of thought. Isn't that just another way of saying—a life of cowardice? Justifying our fears by suggesting we are some-how above the shit of this earth? Argue with a man for five hours, or take five seconds and slice through his left nos-tril—which gets the man's attention better? Which gets him to agree?" (*short pause*) "People like our friend Cicero—they sit in comfort and complain. They sit on their hills in Tusculum and have—conversations. But they are in comfort—because of men like me. I know what the world is like. I know that there are those out there who wish to kill us. And so we must never stop—trying to kill them." (*short pause*) Your letter, Cicero, it's now been copied many times.

CICERO *nods. He isn't surprised.*

It's everywhere. Whatever he touches—he humiliates. Everything.

Long pause. BRUTUS *tries not to cry.*

(*quietly*) It is over. Our Republic. And I hadn't seen that. I had to stand in front of him and have him tell me to my face. To show me. (*short pause*) And I loathe myself. For having been taken in. Having believed—no, for even having hoped. For wanting to believe. And not seeing. How blind could I be? I loathe me.

CICERO: Don't—

BRUTUS: No. The facts were there. I didn't want to see them. Hear them. Think them. I suppose I knew in my gut, which is why—

CICERO: Yes.

BRUTUS: But I grabbed at a straw. That's what I did. And that's what so many of us do. When the truth is—and it is staring us in the face—it is that our "leader" hates every-thing I believe, and believes everything I hate. And there is nothing I can do about that. (*short pause*) We are—pathetic.

BRUTUS *starts to go. He is crying now.*

I think I'm going home. Maybe read a book.

He goes off, leaving PORCIA, *who slowly follows, and then* CIC-ERO, *who is alone.*

Scene 8

A month later; September. Evening. A room in BRUTUS*'s villa, Tusculum.*

SYRUS, *the actor, sits with a box of his "tools of the trade" (pipes, masks, ribbons, etc.). He goes through them, choosing.*

Off: conversation and the occasional laughter.

Pause.

SYRUS *tries out his tools.*

BRUTUS *enters. He looks around the room, moves a stool or chair, etc. He is arranging a performance. Then he hands* SYRUS *some papers.*

BRUTUS: Here.

SYRUS: This is what you told me about?

Nods, then hands him a mask he brought with him.

BRUTUS: And this mask I made myself.

SYRUS *looks it over—there is some resemblance, maybe hair color or hairstyle or eyes—to* BRUTUS *himself.*

SYRUS: Nice. Very nice work. Mouth's wide enough.

BRUTUS: Thank you. Your examples helped.

Some laughter off.

SYRUS: We'll wait until they're finished?

BRUTUS: Between courses. My wife will bring them out soon.

SYRUS *reads the pages* BRUTUS *has given him.*

>(*as* SYRUS *reads*) I very much enjoyed your book, Syrus.
>*The Principles of Theater.* I hadn't— It's much more com-
>plicated than you— When you're just watching. It seems
>easy. (*smiles*) Effortless.

SYRUS: We try.

Short pause as he reads.

>So I didn't completely waste my time in Tusculum.

BRUTUS *is confused.*

>(*explaining*) I wrote the book.

BRUTUS: I see. No you didn't.

SYRUS: (*about the pages*) I won't be able to learn all—

BRUTUS: No. I didn't expect. You just read it. Any questions?

SYRUS: No.

He goes back to his box.

BRUTUS: (*hesitates, then*) I thought there was one idea you didn't talk about—in your book. Something I've been thinking about.

SYRUS: About theater?

BRUTUS: Yes. About . . . It seems to me—that a play can . . . You can say things in a play that—you can't or dare not say in life. Especially given the climate we live in. Things—you might not even want to think.

SYRUS *looks at him.*

SYRUS: Some principles are best not written down. Which doesn't mean they aren't generally understood.

BRUTUS: I see.

PORCIA *enters, leading* CICERO *and* CASSIUS.

CASSIUS: What is this?

CICERO: Where are you taking us?

CASSIUS: I hadn't finished eating.

PORCIA: We'll get back to that.

They see SYRUS.

CICERO: Syrus? I didn't know you were—

BRUTUS: He's staying with us.

SYRUS: I've gone through everyone. Now I'm starting over again.

CICERO: Is this going to be a play?

CASSIUS *has bent down to look through* SYRUS*'s box.*

CASSIUS: (*to* SYRUS) We were just talking about Caesar's entrance into Rome. Talk about theatrics.

SYRUS: (*busy*) I missed it.

CASSIUS: A friend wrote Cicero—said he had giraffes, Gauls, Asiatics, Egyptians, Africans—all in chains. They built a little sea—a lake at the base of the Aventine—to have sea battles.

CICERO: Apparently knocked down a row of decent buildings.

SYRUS: None of you were there?

They shake their heads.

CICERO: Where should we sit? Over here?

BRUTUS: I'll close the shutters.

CASSIUS: It'll get too hot.

BRUTUS: I'll close them. We'll open them later.

He closes the shutters. It gets quite dark.

CICERO: (*to* BRUTUS) What's it going to be about?

CASSIUS: (*to* SYRUS, *as a joke*) So Syrus, is it true that you've bought Cato's villa?

Some laughter.

SYRUS: And where would I find that sort of money?

BRUTUS: Maybe Cicero—

CICERO: Stop it.

BRUTUS: He's rich now.

CASSIUS: (*to* SYRUS) He is.

CICERO: That's not true. And that's not funny.

Short pause.

SYRUS: What . . . ?

CASSIUS: It appears Cicero suddenly received a rather large inheritance. From someone he's never heard of. His debts were paid. A bag of money just arrived.

Short pause.

SYRUS: Caesar?

CICERO: Of course. I'm trying to give it back. No one will take it.

CASSIUS: He owns us all now.

SYRUS: (*to* BRUTUS) I'm ready.

BRUTUS: Take a seat. Right there. (*to* SYRUS) Give me your pipe.

Takes the pipe from SYRUS *and blows in it. All settle down.* POR-CIA *stands to one side and watches.*

I'm the Prologue. (*He begins.*) A man, like many others, is walking alone in the evening.

SYRUS, *now wearing the mask, walks in place.*

Along the gentle hills of a town, one much like this one, Tusculum. But of course it's not Tusculum but has another name. The wind blows. (*He gently blows the pipe.*) And the man walks along thinking out loud, confident that no one can hear . . .

He steps aside.

SYRUS: (*in mask, begins to read the speech* BRUTUS *gave him*) "He who takes away our country. Our Republic. Pits us against ourselves. He who takes away our freedoms and our rights. He who takes away our pride in ourselves and in each other, takes away our moral purpose and resolve. He who corrupts what we cherish. Who divides us to conquer us, who attempts to crown himself and his family 'name.' He—must die."

Pause. SYRUS *turns the page.*

AUTHOR'S NOTE

Conversations in Tusculum is based on real events and people and covers a time, May 45 B.C. to September 45 B.C., that leads up to the assassination of Julius Caesar in March 44 B.C. I have attempted to stay true to the known facts, such as they are, though I have consciously transgressed in three ways: Porcia and Brutus most likely did not marry until June or July 45 B.C., but I have them already married in May. There is no record of Junia Tertia, Cassius's wife and Brutus's half sister, going to Spain to be Caesar's mistress. There are, however, references (including a nasty one by Cicero) that suggest her mother did give her to Caesar at some point, at Caesar's request. And it is recorded that Brutus visited Caesar only once at Caesar's camp during this time, not twice as I have it. And there is no mention of Cassius being with him.

For those who are curious about the performances of plays in wealthy households, Philip Whaley Harsh writes in his introduction to *An Anthology of Roman Drama*: "In the houses or villas of the rich, intimate theaters were frequent. Here troupes might perform mimes or dramas, or a single professional might dance or recite, or the owner or his friends might read their own masterpieces. These private audiences were very different from the public."

The following books proved especially useful in researching the play: M. L. Clarke's *The Noblest Roman: Marcus Brutus and His Reputation*; Anthony Everitt's *Cicero*; Tom Holland's *Rubicon: The Last Years of the Roman Republic*; *Plutarch's Lives* (translations by Rex Warner, John Dryden); F. R. Cowell's *Cicero and the Roman Republic*; Suetonius's *The Twelve Caesars* (Robert Graves translation); F. R. Cowell's *Life in Ancient Rome*; Cicero's *Discussions at Tusculum* (vol. V) (Michael Grant translation); Michael Grant's introduction to *Cicero: On the Good Life*; Michael Foss's *The Search for Cleopatra*; Philip Whaley Harsh's introduction to *An Anthology of Roman Drama*.

And finally:

> *The history of civilization knows few moments equal in importance to the sojourn of Cicero at his houses in the country during the brief period of Caesar's sole rule.*

> —T. Zielinski, scholar quoted in Michael Grant's introduction to *Cicero: On the Good Life*

CPSIA information can be obtained
at www.ICGtesting.com
Printed in the USA
LVHW042102230722
724181LV00009B/433

9 780865 479920